BIRDS, METALS, STONES & RAIN

BIRDS,
METALS,
STONES
& RAIN

Russell Thornton

HARBOUR
PUBLISHING

Harbour Publishing Co. Ltd.
P.O. Box 219, Madeira Park, BC, V0N 2H0
www.harbourpublishing.com

Edited by Silas White
Cover art by Golya Mirderikvand
Cover design by Angela Caravan
Text design by Mary White
Printed and bound in Canada

Harbour Publishing acknowledges financial support from the Government of Canada through the Canada Book Fund and the Canada Council for the Arts, and from the Province of British Columbia through the BC Arts Council and the Book Publishing Tax Credit.

Library and Archives Canada Cataloguing in Publication

Thornton, Russell
    Birds, metals, stones and rain / Russell Thornton.

Poems.
ISBN 978-1-55017-601-8

    I. Title.

PS8589.H565B57 2013   C811'.54   C2013-900212-X

Birds, metals, stones and rain
are mother, father, daughter, son,
birth, death, heaven, hell,
prison, rescue, blindness, sight,
the only time, the only place,
birds, metals, stones and rain.

Contents

I

Squall   11
The Oldest Rock in the World   12
Burrard Inlet Ships   14
Nest of the Swan's Bones   16
The Man Who Sleeps in Cemeteries   18
Greenness   20
The Rain Bush   22
Lead   24
The Envelope   25
The Work of the Creek   26
Triangle   28
North Vancouver Snow   29

II

Rain Wolf, West Coast Trail   33
Palomino   34
Andean Flute   36
River Rainbow   37
When the Big Hand Is on the Starfish   38
The Young Ravens that Cry   40
Cormorants at Lonsdale Quay   42
Lost Rain Casting of a Deer   43
Men Fixing a Roof in the Rain   44
Aluminum Beds   46
How the Alley Crow Ends   48
Flowers   50

III

Book of Sparrows   53
My Daughter and the Seagull's Cry   54
Mykolaiv Bells   56
Arrivals, Departures   58
Perfect Day   60
Playing With Stones   62
My Grandmother's Eyes   63
Blade   64
Aphrodite's Mirror   65
My Daughter and the Geometry of Time   66
Ambleside Beach   68
Gas   70
Iron, a Summary   72
The Praise Tree   73
The Aeschylus Rock   74

Acknowledgements   76
About the Author   79

I

Squall

The clinking becomes a ringing,
solid and clean. The spikes go straight
into the wide earth, the four poles
into the sky. The canvas bells
and flaps, and stays taut in the wind.
That is the tent in a lost camp.

The drumming deepens and quickens.
Wild and intricate, it allows
a melody to break from it,
a mist to lift off it and through.
That is the wet ghost that will ride
along the edges of the flesh.

The plane surface stands brilliant
within the vastness of metal,
and a winged drop of a small bird
flies chirping out of a keyhole.
That is the newborn that unlocks
the clear mirror door of the rain.

The Oldest Rock in the World

A news item: Oldest rocks in the world found on barren Quebec shore

And brought my hand down on the butterfly
And felt the rock move beneath my hand.
  —Irving Layton, "Butterfly on Rock"

In memory of Irving Layton

They look as if they are in mid-tumble
out of the bare and windswept swathe
of outcropping bedrock on Hudson Bay's
eastern shore a one-hour canoe trip
south of Inukjuak. These boulders

of the Nuvvuagittuq greenstone belt—
four and a third billion years old,
dating back to a mere three hundred
million years after the globe formed
out of a cloud of cosmic debris and dust.

When the planet was being pummelled
by meteors, comets and asteroids,
microbes interacted with iron
in the primordial seas and emerged
as Earth's very earliest life,

and nestled in sediment and wrote
their bio signature in the rust that fills
these boulders' creases. Now beyond
the treeline, beyond houses, the boulders
have sat longer than the combined lifespans

of countless generations of animals—
far longer than human history
and any dreaming of the way within rock
or of a dying back to when only rock
framed what would be wind for human breath.

Now the microbe might bless us. Allow
us to stand trembling in bright, bright light.
Witness our core, the one annunciation.
Hear us: from out of the depths have we
called thee, from out of our will and wonder—

the doors in us so closed, we think the door
to rock is shut. We cannot die or love enough—
and love, though it brings us to its door
and unlocks it for us, will not follow—
and our signatures nestle in time and we

forget them. Wind is in a hand of force
that wraps around wind, and the rock has moved
and taken our hand, our hand made of nothing
other than what the rock is made of—
in death we lose nothing that is not

of the death and life of this rock. The wind
moves endlessly, and the rock moves around
the wind, and the planet moves around
the wind and around the sun, and around
everlasting cosmic debris and dust.

Wind is rushing through the oldest place
we have named. The song it sings is learning
itself, beginning and ending with Earth.
More names than we can know are rushing through,
and within the names the rock is opening.

Burrard Inlet Ships

At a window overlooking water—container ships
and bulk carrier ships lying at anchor
framed in front of us. *They're always there,*
I hear a voice say. As if the ships were the same ships
that sat there twenty-four or forty-eight hours ago.
As if, in the middle of the night, the ships did not
arrive and drop anchor at exact latitudes and longitudes.
And tugboats did not come and bring the ships to dock,
and other ships not arrive and take the first ships' places—
in the middle of the night. As if the ships were not
emptied of what they brought here and loaded up again
while the ships' sailors took their hours' shore leave
to go to a bank, visit a doctor, talk with a priest,
buy a blouse or bracelet for a woman back home.
As if, between sundown and dawn, the ships did not depart.
And every two or three days, a new ship and new crew
did not sit at each terminal wharf. As if it was not
now a new ship visible outside the window.
All night, out on the water, the ships' horns send out
sound signals for their arrivals and departures,
and all night, in inlet-filling fog, the ships' horns
send out long blasts, long repeating notes—accompaniment
to the circuit of sleep in the houses along the shore.
New ships and crews come, new products are brought
from faraway locales, and new loads of coal, sulphur,
lumber and wheat are taken to faraway locales.
All night, when gulls come up from the inlet
through cloud and rain, gull after gull takes up
the same insane-sounding cry of unfathomable
emergency in a wilderness of water, and circles with the same
single message that seems wound and unwound
as on a wire anchored somewhere unknown to any gull
in the inlet circling and circling through its tides.

All night, the outsized ships come and go—all night.
As if they were not, each of them, the same ship powering
over the glowing deep blue water-globe. As if the voice
at this window had not been with me all along,
waiting inside my hearing. As if it was not
the voice of one more myself than I can know.
As if this one's home had not always been here
where he could see an anchor-place and hear gulls.

Nest of the Swan's Bones

She will build a nest of the swan's bones...
  —Robinson Jeffers, "Shiva"

High in the blue air above the dumpster in the back lane,
between the mountains and the tidal flats,
on the thermals and updrafts a summer hawk does slow turns.

The crows pick at the waste on the asphalt.
The men push jingling shopping carts. Or stand and mimic life
in a prison yard. The wild white swan is dead. Where I caught

trout as a child, no trout swim now. The drives
and crescents gouge ravines, make creeks disappear. Where wild
baby fish run, they run the gauntlet of penned fish. They are eaten alive,

their eyes popping out as sea lice feed inside their heads.
The hawk dances. Circles, dances. Its shadow flits
unnoticed across men, spreads over a rodent or bird

it dives to, inserts claws into, and clamps large feet on, stomping it
as if beating time. It splays flesh and flies
away with it into sunlight. The hawk takes up an owl's hoot

and a sparrow's last chirp, a heron's bill-snap and a smelt's silence
into its disinterested scream. The swan
glides in beauty in the hawk's sight, and fills all the hawk sees

with brilliant, blinding whiteness. Moment by moment,
the men go back and forth. They search out anything they can trade
for a full bottle or syringe or pipe. In my room with the lit-up screen,

I lie and dream my dream. I feel it must also be God's,
this dream of the person of persons. Where the dream comes through,
it punctures me, and I breathe dark air. The air thuds

into pockets like a plummeted elevator. O monster home. O
specialty wine outlet. O auto mall. The wild white swan
is dead. The hawk hunts and kills the swan for love. It will build a new

nest of the swan's bones. It will keep this nest unseen.
I am a person. I soil the cage in which my heart flings
and flings itself against the bars. I try to own

the view of every murderer, and yet I try to sing
the way out through the hawk's claw-holes to the repose
in the nest of fire at the tip of the hawk's wing.

The Man Who Sleeps in Cemeteries

Refuse recyclable paper yard-bags. Refuse gloves.
Collect yard trimmings the way you know how—
I'll do likewise. My friend, don't hurt your head.
Afternoons, slide down the avenue. At every intersection,
karate kick crosswalk buttons. Show up mornings
a very macho character, a little threatening. Show up
fawning, a little flirtatious. Talking religion, bitches.
Going on about your lady—in the mirror, lipsticked.

Gang boy in Colombia. Gang man. You left that life.
Yes, they found you in Miami. They killed your wife,
your two kids, they threw you off a balcony. Now lay
down your head. With strands of yourself off in the trees,
running quiet and clear in the quick creek water.

With your arms wrapped around surgical scars.
With your collection of scars. Miami to Vancouver? *I think
I walked.* Lay down your English. *Por favor!* Scowl
and explain to me in Spanish that you don't speak
Spanish anymore. Or Portuguese. Or the Quebec French
that jumps out of you. Explain to me that North Vancouver
has the most beautiful cemetery you've ever slept in.
No landlords, no need to pull a knife. With the different
parts of your brain in the right places, explain it.

With your jumble of words, lay down your head.
With your jumble of words. With your single joint
per day and the pain gone out of your skull. Let
the sections of your head click into a proper machined fit.

Yes, killed so many times, scattered in so many places,
you can't say—say a loud *Fuck you!* in the direction
of your every past boss. Say it at your every Refugee Board
hearing, at your every income assistance interview.
Consult the cemetery's visiting bear, coyote and deer.
Consult the community of the dead flowing in unison
beneath your head. Then make your many decisions
and rule the parts of your head. My friend, my co-worker,
here's a coffee, a set of garden tools and plastic yard-bag.
Come do your expert work. Whistle all day the songs
that came to you in the night through the cold clean dirt.

Greenness

What am I now that I was then
    —Delmore Schwartz, "Calmly We Walk Through This April's Day"

I turn to grass tufts and see unsullied
clear greenness displaying its steel. I see
what I should see, simple close-mown spring grass
like that of any suburban house lawn.
I turn again and decades disappear
and I see the dark grass all down the block—
I wake, run out of a basement and go
reeling across yard after wide yard. Here,
I unlock a gate. Swing it open. Go
to a neighbour's front door. I knock, and ask
for help. But I am still half in the house
where I crouch, and we gaze at each other,
my mother and I, while my father holds
her so she will burn in the fireplace flames—
it is only a pretend me who asks.
Here, a woman blankets me and leaves me
in a den. The simple grass I turn to
is of the same greenness that pierces me
where I sit in a deep plush chair and hear
a man on a phone, sink and right away
begin to dream of grass. Lawns touch my bare
feet with cold dew and make me swift, shoot me
full of starlight the grass stores in its maze
of roots and make me shine bright. Here, I slip
out of the blanket, the den, and go back
outside and down the rows of blades all
waiting to take me in. What I bring,
I bring to grass to help it find its way
beyond every house. I turn to grass
that is close-mown, sunlit in the morning,

and turn to the grass that rinses my eyes
wide for the dark. When the soft spring rain flows
busy through grass, the always houseless night
helps continue this beginning. When grass
lengthens and men come to cut it, I laugh
with the laughing greenness. Unknown heaven
in its depth in the grass, once here cannot
be unmade. What I am now that I was
then can only be what is in grass—here
in what reaches breathing, reaching nowhere
but from blade to blade. It breathes and is iron
that is not cast by anyone but grows.

The Rain Bush

*...and, behold, the bush burned with fire, and the bush
was not consumed. And Moses said, I will now turn aside,
and see this great sight...*
   —Exodus 3: 2–3

I heard kindlings, full flames, a furnace fire
and singing ore. I turned aside and saw
rain blowing into the branches of a bush—
the molten metal cooling, magnetic,
its memory of directions, its brilliant
dream of Earth come back. The bush stood—
living, intricate, a hollow sphere lit
in a theatre blackness with circling
mirror-drops. New wind arrived, and the array
of branches swerved on the stalk, and the bush
caught new rain, was still again, and the mirrors
continued circling, losing their silver
and becoming glass. So whatever a mirror
displayed through the air was as soon released,
whatever memory it let appear
in any image as soon disappeared—
in the mirror a rememberer could meet
himself in immediate new transparency
haloed in haze and glitter. Each mirror,
as it arrived, resolved itself in multiple
weddings of gazes, in gazes dying
into waiting gazes. The entire bush
was a changing mask, radiant with desire,
charged with identity, and turning aside
with what is given to us. The mask said:

our unremembering, when we turn aside
to what turns to us, and are nothing
of what we have been—that is the gift of all
we can desire. That is to hear our names
spoken clearly, and look and see no one.
That is to know a voice, and know the voice
is an elsewhere saying we are what is not us,
while the elsewhere brings rain, pours bright
ore into our always darkening day.

Lead

Don't kill me, father!
  —Euripides, *Herakles*

Freshly cut, it is bluish white.
It tarnishes in the moistness
of air to grey. The grey allows
the black to show through. The first dose
drowns the original anger
in bright bliss. The next doses take
the anger, hide it, increase it,
make it indistinguishable
from what is now the dark; is now
the brother of need. No way back
to try to stand and see that change.
Or imagine I will save you,
my father, before or after
you are like a man whose eyes roll
in his head and who releases
lead-tipped arrows into his sons.
Those sons move like slow birds and fall.
The sky they look out at narrows
and then there is no sky. No way
back to where I see clear, intact,
even my memory of you.
I am neither cursed nor favoured.
I drink what you drank in my heart
that drinks blood and time, while it stays
lodged in me, lustreless metal,
hate not mine and mine, resisting
corrosion, conducting nothing,
and I carry the weight of it.
I simply carry it, with eyes
that carry light. I carry it.

The Envelope

The thrilled, cold arm flying. It finds the slid-
open living room window. The hand takes hold
of the set of blinds and bangs the metal

again and again against the main pane and sill.
It is my father. He has not visited me in years.
He brings horizontal rain, numerous blades

that he allows to snick and swipe and flash.
Whatever I think years are for, years swerve
through on the entering wind he brings. Whatever

my hearing is for, I hear nothing but wind.
He has gotten into the building and is in the corridor.
All night, he knocks and bangs on the door. Father,

I hear myself say, I am now a middle-aged man,
with young children in my care, and it is too late
for me to answer. And father, if I let you in,

I would crush your skull the way some men will
an intruder's, some an enemy's, some a boy's.
The blinds, the wind and rain, are actual

banging blinds and wind and rain—before I fall
more asleep, I know it. Still, I want with all my heart,
whatever my heart is, to go to the door,

and am laid out and paralyzed. The knocking stops.
He slips an envelope under the door and is gone.
It stays in my dream, and stays unopened.

The Work of the Creek

The rain falls delicate, cold. It touches to the creek—
twinklings swaying out across water
as if rays have arrived from a womanly star.

There in the creek depths, in the runoff
that has crushed itself into a clear, calm flow—
dark, wavering reflections, bough on bough.

Now I know how, if I have been anywhere,
I have been full of another—that person
and no other. It is a place and is an instant

pouring with a perpetual prophecy—
two people may meet their twin essences
in each other, terrible, tender ones,

who turn together in the deep green beds
at the end of all that separates them,
and are the mirror in front of which they disappear.

The sound of the rain falling meets the sound
of a prayer unfamiliar to me rising
within my spine into my skull. I touch my brow

to the trunk of a fir. The prayer leaves me
and is the stand of bright, black creek-bank trees.
The quickening creek mist moves over my face.

I watch the water slide past, something in it
of every love that has ever been—
the creek a raindrop the creek counts, forgets,

counts, forgets again. What two people know
to be all there is, is what they cannot know.
My eyes are the bandages of my eyes.

Triangle

My child points and points, and makes her baby sounds.
Her first cry rang the hospital room air
and entered my skull and stayed there, echoing.
I lie in bed and feel my chest seize up, besieged
by time, my senses multiply and my memories
leave me as if I have become one of my dead.
The apartment is a raft. There is limitless wind,
directionless vast rising and collapsing waves,
and enough to eat and drink but no arrival
at any shore. I hear my child cry and I turn
to listen for her first *Daddy* as if that word
could comfort both of us. A gull cries, my child points
out the window glass into the dark, her cry joins the wind,
and she turns to me the crushed clear quartz of her eyes.
The gull and me and herself, she makes this her triangle.
For me there is her, the world, and my dead
among the dead, and this is my triangle. Her cry
rings it like the musical instrument but invisible.
And some of the dead will sing and not be heard
except as gull cries. And some of the living
will lose the way to their own pain, forget it,
know as if for the first time the pains in the world
in the midst of its appetite and slaughter, know
the child's name they say points to all they see.

North Vancouver Snow

Out the window the grey-blue air. Elation in the sheen.
The mountains and new-made clouds gather and gather.
The baby being born pauses. The sky casts itself
in precise quietness. Four in the afternoon. Five.
The hour is tracing itself back through the whorls
of the fetus fingertips to all hours. Finally he's here,
making the voices in the hospital room rhyme
in his presence, bringing with him the clue that finds us,
the dark blue metal of his eyes. The fine cold
is organizing the water within the clouds. His eyes
are half-designing the sight of what is now out the window,
though he can see only the blur of the close faces,
the day's late light circling through the metal
and searching through the invisible forge of the air
and finding the falling flakes of the year's first snow.

January 14, 2012

II

Rain Wolf, West Coast Trail

It is standing at the edge
of a clearing, pale glacial
eyes narrow and lined in black,
the wolf's kohl. The entire wolf
the thick kohl of my own eyes,
it brings jagged grey trees, stones
lying alive on the ground, rain
like a bead-curtained doorway,
steel wool cloud and the dark's sheen
sharp into my eyes. Without
any flaw in its fury,
a wolf of antimony,
eater of impurities,
it eats the decrepit king
of my eyes and a reborn
king emerges from a fire,
the burned wolf hissing like rain
and shaking away the ash.
The trees have burned up, the wolf
lifts its nose to smoke, charcoal,
and licks the visible clean,
leaving the two pinpoint lights
of its eyes in the dawn air.

Palomino

Light angles in through a block of bramble
and the small horizontal rectangle
ground-level window. Rough rock to the glass,
rock ledge layered in dust. I work here
in the dimness at a bench with a six-
by-three-inch stray piece of half-inch-thick steel
and a plastic toy horse in mid-high stride.
Glue the hooves to the pedestal. Paint black
the entire body, let it dry, paint on
metallic silver patches. Then the rays
entering the basement slender and pale
halt, gather in the animal outline,
grow brilliant, and complete a first horse,
its colouring and proportions exact.
When we were with my father, I would take
down his encyclopedia volume
and find colour plates of horses. Trace them,
pencil crayon in the palominos'
tawny patches. I descend now to hunch
like an old man half-ghost and see a horse
hardly ever visible in the sky
appear in front of me, an offspring foal
flashing as distinct and bright a silver
as the stars that show winged Pegasus
the father in flight. See the horse, the hide
the black of space, harnessed only in light
decorating it wildly with splashes,
take the new gift of itself to the sire,
to the farthest away reaches of life,
and appear again, a painted plaything
held in a workbench vice. The air the bit
of death in its mouth, that Equuleus,

that little horse of the constellations,
flits with the rays into the basement dark,
dust falling deep over the long roads home.

Andean Flute

The breath of light in my bones when I write the word earth.
   —Alejandra Pizarnik, "In a Copy of *Les Chants de Maldoror*"

The same way small winds come,
new air out of the dark, discoverers,
voices of first ones, chirpers,
only through the dense core, mantle, crust,
only through the bulks of animals
and their roars and cries, through
the circle of mountains rising
to Machu Picchu, only through
these could they have come—
the birds beyond our sight in the sun,
singing for no reason but to sing,
the singing a travelling of a song
with no beginning and no end.
Only through our falling lives
could they have come, our lives made
of the words we most want to say,
and the words made of the knowing
that there is more love in matter
than we can utter, only through
the bones within us writing the word earth
to no one, nothing, but the earth,
only through these could they have come—
birds arriving and departing
and arriving and departing, wing beats
keeping time with heartbeats, the pause
between heartbeats the breath of light
that stays and is the earth and is the flute.

River Rainbow

My two-year-old is standing on the swath
of pebbles piled alongside the pale green
and the bright white of the river that rides
down out of the canyon to run level
and free to the inlet. She's throwing stones
into stray pools and eddies. Looking up,
saying to the air *boohewun, boohewun*
for the dozens of gulls. Dipping her hand
into the cold water for coloured stones,
throwing them, watching them splash. Then saying
again, *boohewun.* Looking up at me
with the grey-blue of the river heron,
one of its feathers fallen into her eyes.
She looks back to the water. Throws a stone
and adds circles within widening circles.
Throws another stone and her irises
halo the river flow. Throws another
and in her pupils the heron opens
its wings and lifts to arc through the blackness
lit blue. Now airborne over the water,
draws the halo out into a rainbow.
The gulls hosanna with their shrieks. She throws
a new stone, a new rainbow, a wild iris
of continuous colours. Any name
she utters is a rainbow, any bird
she sees is a *boohewun*, a messenger
carrying to her a name for a rainbow,
a heron, and bringing her a heron's blue.

When the Big Hand Is on the Starfish

When the big hand is on the starfish
and the little hand is on the crab, you're looking up
at the lobby clock. It's six o'clock. Now a flock
of sea-green Canada geese, the sun's rays
blazing over it, flies past a mass of sea life—
lobsters, turtles, sea snails, skate, make their way
through forests of seaweed. This is outside,
within the arched entranceway. Seahorses, pufferfish,
traced in terracotta, swim the front wall face
as they would along inlet shore rock. The same biplane
flies by twice, three times, then the same Zeppelin—
here, it is and always will be 1930,
when this was the tallest edifice in the entire
British Commonwealth. When the big hand
is on the starfish and the little hand
is on the lobster, it's three o'clock. Boats and ships
go by—the *Resolution,* the *Golden Hind*,
the HMS *Egeria,* the *Sonora*, the *Empress of Japan*.
Inside again, at the five brass elevator doors,
above which sailing vessels burst out of waves
with lighting in their prows, stand five female
elevator operators, chosen for their beauty,
wearing sailor uniforms, female usherers
into hardwood interiors like ships' cabins—
1930 is also 2009, and now they're the flowing light
that chooses the lobby's stained glass windows
for their beauty, and the zodiac pictured
on the polished marble floor. When the big hand
is on the starfish and the little hand
is on the turtle, it's two o'clock. Terracotta
Canada geese fly along the building's sides
to meet above the brass-framed main glass doors.

This is the Marine Building, address 355
on a street named for Sir Harry Burrard,
ex-shipmate of the captain who, at the behest
of His Majesty's Royal Navy, sailed here
to find a mysterious sea route, and failed,
yet mapped the area's every intricate coastal mile.
When the big hand is on the starfish
and the little hand is on the sea snail, it's nine o'clock,
and I'm nine, or is it seven, years old, turning
the page in Haig-Brown's *Captain of the Discovery*
where the captain and a dozen of his crew
sail in the ship's yawl through the tree-branch-
overhung narrows into the inlet. People
from the nation whose home is the north shore
put off in canoes to greet them and offer
freshly cooked smelts. The Englishman at once
orders his men to shorten sail and allow
the canoes to keep pace. Now he looks out
across the inlet—which he will name for Sir Harry.
The geese that fly across his sails, and past
the bright brass buttons on George Vancouver's
blue naval coat, fly now through the brass rays
brightening the Marine Building entranceway
and framing a *Discovery*. When the big hand
is on the starfish and the little hand is on the crab,
it's six o'clock again. For an instant,
or is it a lifetime, terracotta geese pass
into living geese and back again—art deco.
They pass through where illustrious ships
sail by and famous buildings stand. They pass
through to living geese like the seahorses pass
through to living seahorses, like the starfishes
to those with feet fastening onto rock,
purple arms slowly decorating time.

The Young Ravens that Cry

The trees here twist the ocean up through the night of their roots
and let it burn away out of their arms into the day.
The raven rides the repeating croak and call

of its shining-eyed need and demand. The animal that hates
carries his old expulsion as far as he can,
and arrives at a new paradise. His God loves him

even when he lays down pipelines, launches tankers,
exudes sadness and shame. His God keeps in sight
the huddled fledglings, touches the slenderest hair,

while the raven turns its young early out of its high nest,
and the young call for food from a mother that does not exist,
vanished into the blackness of their wings.

The raven's other call, a rainforest's soft, rhythmic bell,
Elijah heard when the flock fed him near a brook.
Tales retell themselves like returning waves—

here tiny-skulled shore birds wander bitumen-slicked.
The heirs of eternity eat royal food, cry
thinking the Holy Spirit is speaking in them. Unclean

flesh, blood, bone and black feathers, the raven
tries to see everything on the shore, scavenges, cries alone.
The raven that flew off with the ball of light

that it found hidden in black box within black box
tears open a bewildered black shore bird,
picks through to the heart and finds food. The animal

that hates looks out over the ocean at the sun
and sees into the black boxes of his heart. In the last box
the dark-raying bird of the sun, the God turned out of the nest,

is feasting on him like carrion. He hears no grieving cry
for the gap he makes in the creation or for the shore
beautiful as at its first sunrise when he darkens it.

* Cherith Brook is where the prophet Elijah was fed by ravens *(1 Kings 17)*.

* The black box containing the ball of light that illuminates the world, and the old man's daughter as beautiful as hemlock fronds at sunrise—are elements of the Haida myth of the raven who steals the light.

Cormorants at Lonsdale Quay

Black flock, long curved black necks, long black beaks,
torsos belling out against the cold grey-blue,
they roost along the SeaBus dock roof,
feast on the small fish in the inlet. They drop in groups
to the water, dive, reappear, lift and sit
on top of the large shore rocks. Each is a device
with wings turning on a cardinal point in the back bone,
opening and closing as a pair of bone leaves
joined through a knuckle by a smooth bone pin.
Each is a set of hinges allowing doors of air to swing wide.
Producing a sound like that of construction work,
they cannot sing like other birds but simply cry
their labour, carrying an axis inside
as if carrying the earth's cardinal point
to countless locations. They fly down and back—
wings hinging wave spray that flashes blinding bone-
white across the black rock. The spray is a door opening
while gravity holds the waters around the earth
and the tides move in and out, in and out.

Lost Rain Casting of a Deer

I

The waters of the runoff surge through the ravine, an unending succession of lightning strikes, the mist drives down between the steep banks and the trees, the rain shuts its vault. The creek shakes the skeleton of its rock course shooting along skull after skull. The waters become a liquid natural wax. The wax moves smooth and quick into mouths open to receive it, letting it fill the mould.

II

Curved white edges of creek ripples cut away the confine. The entire creek pulls itself into the body of a leaping raincloud-coloured animal. The moments that animal of wax is encased and melted out are the moments the iron oxides, charcoal and oils of the first paintings run wet on the walls of caves illuminated by fires, the colours still deepening within the bounding outlines.

III

Dark grains of the unencumbered musk pod flow out with the creek's lost and shapeless wax, and over the waters faceless as the first waters. The creek mist thickens. The musk it is carrying of ravine leaves, glacial till and ozone thickens. Metals present at the beginning melt, and the alloy rushes again into the mould it finds, and that finds it, within the shifting vacancies and probabilities.

IV

The living deer stepped out into the envelope of a clearing in the mountaintop mist, its eyes glittering soft black, the way a sculpture arrives, the mould removed, the polished bronze undraped. But this deer melted into mist leaving the blackness that poured in its eyes, and in the blackness its scent, the sweetness of copper, the nullity of tin, and the musk of the rain that was always the traveller.

Men Fixing a Roof in the Rain

Up on top of the stack of window squares
each with a person at a desk and screen,
two men in yellow slickers and hard hats,
weighty toolkits strapped around their middles,
work with measuring tapes and lengths of steel
on the flat roof of City Hall. Wind, rain
and seagulls veering past, the two workmen
do what they do. Like quiet windup toys,
they go to and fro, turn at right angles,
power-saw the lengths, place them down, figure
the spacing between the rows, and set out
the support frame for a new roof surface.
The wind and rain increase, the travelling
low heavens press down on the men's hard hats,
the men fix the frame in place. The seagulls
continue to veer, crows flap, past. The men
now stand side by side and survey their work.
They have measured, cut, put in the right place
what they were supposed to put in place; they
intend their work to stay. The two of them
look like little children gazing out across
a play mat or a park sandbox. Except
children will assemble a world with blocks
and shape fantastical grotesqueries
with sunlit mud and immediately,
gleeful and laughing loud, topple it. When
the roof fails of its own accord or when
the poison winds arrive and the window
glass explodes and hot rain flies, the chances
are that somewhere men will be performing
this same rooftop work. Somewhere other men
will be walking back and forth and standing
proud in costly suits or archaic robes
handing out or reaching out for awards
in front of crowds. And as from the beginning,

the real parts of the world will be whispering—
but now they will be whispering more and more
of how all this while it is being destroyed.

Aluminum Beds

When he pulls up in a truck and hefts new beds
into the house to replace our camp cots,
we see the dark in a metal's dull sheen
is the dark displayed in his beard. The sound
rushing through the hollows of the square posts,
the frames, guards and rails, is the sound rushing
through the spaces he has made within us.
He sets them all down, the pieces he measured,
sheared, and welded together in the evenings
in his father's factory, while I, half hidden
in among the machines, gathered up scrap
fallen to the cement floor. The four beds
stand in our shared room, one for each of us—
with this he fulfills his unwanted office.
He leaves us soon after, and I keep vigil.
Nightly I allow not one of my brothers
to speak or even audibly breathe. I know
that the sound of any of our young voices
will distract the light trying to make its way
through the fitted substance of the metal. I know
at the same time that this light is my father
searching for his sons. He does not know it—
long before he left us, his love began travelling
to us apart from him. If I memorize him,
I will be able to see the love. If I cut
from myself all that is not my love for him,
the right set of rays will find us. My brothers
fall asleep one by one. I lie and wait
for my dream. There is no space not swirling,
no fire with its core of blackness not burning,

within the beds' angular emptiness
because of the love meant for us. Through the night,
the metal embraces me. It is a skeleton,
unending silver, pure and cold, and I become it,
the light of my father's love arrived at last.

How the Alley Crow Ends

The outsized crow flaps down its purple-black,
it caws down past a power-chiselling man
and puts its feet onto spat-up asphalt.
The cawing speeds up. The alley keeps on breaking,
the cawing keeps on describing the crow,
it speeds up. The crow circles, arrogant, eye
angled at the jackhammer, wings the colour
and sheen of an oil spill. The overfull
dumpster stinks in the hot sun. The crow comes
with its jerking, cawing head down the flyway
of birds dead and living. It comes bowlegged,
fluffing up its feathers into a mane
to show off. Comes with its black breast ragged
as if it has garlanded itself in the pelts
of the sparrows and robins it has eaten.
The chunks of asphalt keep on rolling up. The crow
vacates its ground for a telephone pole,
goes now from pole to pole, cable to cable,
high gutter to high gutter. It flouts the rows
of the alley crosses as it would the trio
on any storied hill. Its own iridescent
darkness in the middle of the day. The cawing
speeds up, it increases to full volume
the brute static of its beating signal,
the alley flow of horrible noise. My daughter cries
for music—*CD! CD!* The crow caws
with wet strings dangling from its beak. The rot
drifts up and down the alley. While the lids
in the good yards stay closed tight. My daughter cries
for me to lift her up. The crow observes us
from a pole opposite. Men file down the alley
with supermarket carts and look oil-slicked
in the burning receipt of the sun. The cawing
speeds up. The sun nails the men to the alley,

breaks their legs at the knees and pulls them down
off the crosses of its rays and they disappear.
My daughter repeats *Up! Up!* to see the heights
of the swaying trees. The alley crows nest there
in rough rings of sticks. Now I see my father
hurt out of the reach of repair. It was if a crow
took and held him in its beak like garbage
and uttered him, death hilarious. I recall
the last I was to hear of his voice, the insult
issuing down a phone line, the caw. My daughter
cries again for music. Music of running,
almost flying, on soft grass green beyond green
and the sky deep-glowing blue, the sea rocking
and the clean sand silver in the wash of waves.
The crow's caw jackhammers the heat-laden
alley air and now the dark comes and the crow
is gone. The silence after the final caw
is the silence inside my daughter's cry.

Flowers
for Dora

No one could resist the charm in her bright black eyes.
The townspeople called her Little Maria.

You explained how her parents sent her out
to steal flowers she would then sell in the streets.

Now she was circling lightly through the bar
like an emissary, holding out a bouquet.

Had I drunk too much Greek wine, or had I seen
the same vivid Aegean-coloured flowers before—

left by the relatives who had come before us
to the graveside I visited with you that morning.

It was a year ago today, you had told me,
that you leaned over and closed your grandmother's blue eyes.

III

Book of Sparrows

I

Fly, fly, okay, okay, she says.
I lift her up to the cold
window and she sees sparrows
appear and disappear.
Hiding, hiding, she says,
laughing, chirping, as if she knows
they are taken care of in their lives
in the trees and in the air.

II

I go get it, I go get it, she says.
I let her down and she runs
to a book and opens it to where
sparrows sit on a summer branch.
Light is finding her eyes, new,
wise as an old woman's. The one
who calls out with her voice
is only barely hiding in her.

My Daughter and the Seagull's Cry

The cries come sharp, deep as the night and bright;
they tear the dark in my ear. It is the gulls
that have come up from the inlet through the still air,
the first proprietors of the daylight. The cries
rush out through the single narrow way of all their throats.
My daughter's favourite among her first words:
seagull. Then *I seagull.* She remembered
the white-winged ones that came clamouring and flocking
where she stood on the sand at the sea edge. The sweet
crystalline cry poured from her as she went up
on her toes and flung her arms about and gull after gull
arrived and circled close and cried into the circle
of soft lightning they had made around her.
My daughter's first nightmare: standing at the crib bars,
eyes fixed wide yet still dreaming, not knowing
where she was, repeating again and again
her bottomless cry. The cry as full of address
as the cries of the lovers in the next apartment
calling out wordless across the sudden distances,
a calling almost unearthly. As full of address
as the final cry of abandonment on the cross.
The gulls' cries come sharp, and gulls come wheeling
up from the water as if on reconnaissance
and searching for what they have lost, not knowing
what it is they have lost though they carry it
as they perform every wing-thrust, every glide.
They fly their torsos, beaks, eyes; they are alive and yet
they are desperate ghosts, their cries scavenging cries.
They wake her now, one cry then another
like wild beings in the room, and immediately
my daughter shouts *seagull,* as if a dream
has been waiting within her to put the word in her mouth
at just this instant. In her two-year-old voice

she takes her ecstatic run out to meet
the gull's sound with her word and runs out into all
the words that will ever come to find her,
even the word that is her own name. Like a hand
through a window, they will come to snatch her away.
The sea waves will arrive, hushed and radiant,
rolling her first cry in their foam. The flock's cries
will collect up the world, opening it like a door.

Mykolaiv Bells

In the planted, tree-swayed back garden
in the hot late summer sun—
I hadn't thought it would be hot here,
or the fine, baked earth rich
with ripe peppers, tomatoes,
hazelnuts, walnuts, pears, plums, apples, grapes.

I had imagined a cold plain,
not a voluptuousness, not a subtle,
various fertility, not a flirtatiousness.

I thought now of vineyard-crowded
corners of Bulgaria, Macedonia, Thessaly—
this deep-lit air around the delicate vines,
its flitting, swinging, insubstantial gold.

I hadn't thought I would hear bells here—
rhythmic bell-clatter while I lay half-sleeping
in the garden in the morning. Near-East-
sounding to me—not East-European.
And the earth itself
keeping time. Clanging,
calling the sun close, calling the grapes—
so the wine could arrive, clear gold,
in its cupboardful of old bottles.

How did we find each other? you asked—
on the poor bed and couch
of that den-like house, and as you walked in
through the low doorway, across
the small, astonishingly bright threshold,
tall and slender, hair draping you.

The whole morning, a garden filling
with echoing bell-ringing, bell-music
I listened after, wanting more and more of it.

While I lay and read in the afternoon,
I looked up to see different-coloured cats leap
lazily from a fence onto the house.

Then, in the night, we heard weasels, come
out of hiding in the garden, or out
of some other garden—quick gong-drumming
of their feet as they ran the sloped roof.

Late morning, potatoes and wine
on a rough kitchen counter—
set out because it was what there was.
Wine that seemed to be ringing
within its gold—looking out
at us from simple glasses.

Arrivals, Departures

First a guarded corridor, then fifty feet
of floor and different glass walls between us—
me arrived, waiting for you, you detained,
passport and visa from the wrong country
confiscated, luggage and plane ticket
confiscated, flight back home changed.
There you were in your multi-coloured
homemade coat, a slender Slavic Venus,
Tartar cheekbones, brilliant yet soft blue eyes,
troubling the *frontiera polizia.*
After a while, we were having a shared dream—
a week of me on one side of a world, you
on the other side, where all you could do
was walk around and around in circles,
then try to sleep curled up off in a corner,
as you tried to avoid the guards and their taunts.
In your country, you grace a theatre—
here it is assumed you are a visiting *prostitute,*
and I your pimp. We become two humans
trapped in separate clear containers,
still trying to join by instinct, slipping
and falling, again and again. Two children
trying to climb opposite sides of a hill
of sand that only sweeps us lower. Two numbers
trying to occur together and solve an equation.
No point in mouthing words back and forth—
it is too far away for either of us to see.
But you reach out and frame my face. I realize
I am blowing kisses to someone. You forced
to live in a part of an airport for five days—
the first three days without food. Me forced
to make appeals to officials who ignore me.
Finally, I put a bribe into the right hand—
I am let through to cross from *bella Italia*
into a departure lounge. We can say nothing,

but twine ourselves around each other
across airport seats for an hour, allowed
entry into a silence we now know in ourselves,
making a place of no arrival or departure.

Perfect Day

Three days before your ninetieth birthday
was her eighty-fourth birthday.
A couple of the staff brought a cake
to the table where you had your meals
and sang "Happy Birthday" to her,
and touched gently at her head
so she would blow in the direction
of the half-dozen candles.
Then you got up from your chair
to sing to her too,
and in a moment of lucidity
asked those present, *What do you think
of my eighty-four-year-old bride?*
My grandmother, wide eyes
unable to see you, tear-filled,
leant over and kissed you.

There were second and third cups
of coffee for her to drink
as she talked with her friends,
and after a while, tired,
you went slowly by yourself
up to the rooms the two of you shared
and had a stroke, and lay down,
and two or three hours later,
your whole family around you,
your power of speech gone,
your last words uttered, died.

With the memory you had left,
when you saw the cake and heard the song
you realized it was your wife's birthday—
and maybe in a part of yourself
found the way to the completion
of the gift you had promised her
sixty-odd years before,
and decided this was as it should be,
it was the perfect day.

Playing With Stones

When I carry her home each evening
from the park playground swing, she pleads with me
to let her walk on the bed of smooth stones
at the front of our apartment building.
She wants to find individual stones
and put them in her wide pocket, then place
the same stones along a row of large rocks.
I would like us to stay as we are now
within the flowering and flowing gold
gaze of the sun's late rays. And suddenly
I imagine a day when she is old.
As if I were her child and she was soon
to be gone, I begin to grieve for her,
little mother, my daughter. Carrying
her shepherdess's bag filled with her stones,
one for each sheep in her flock, already
she is keeping count for when it is night
and she brings the sheep into the stone fold,
already she is asking that they all
be kept in the great invisible scrip.
The tears she comes to cry for those she loves,
the tears others who love her cry for her,
will stray and go lost, so she places stones
one by one on flat rock, stones that are tears
she gathered as they rolled out of the sun.

My Grandmother's Eyes

The leaves of last summer
that danced their green light
through the lifting trees
lie changed and scattered now,
dull pennies on the path
melting coldly into the earth.
Her eyes, her old eyes,
that shone and were pale green,
the green of the river water
as it flows in mist and sun
to meet the deep inlet,
have turned colour like leaves
now that sight has fallen away.
Where once her gaze was wide
and danced with all it took in,
now there is a hung head and fear,
and she looks down at nothing,
suddenly stares out at nothing.
Soon her eyes will have become
more than even she has seen,
but until then her drained eyes
are pennies laid over her eyes.

Blade

I

Razor-edged steel. I lean and concentrate
what strength I possess, worshipful. Keep the blade
inserted in under another man's jaw.
Keep it exactly there. Close around our heads,
the same original and ultimate means
as within us, blackness, now a halo—
the blade the only light. I observe his face,
the unyieldingness in the glance, and realize
he is my father, and he and I are here
to perform this act together and know it
as our single embrace. If I lapse, he will
be able to kill me. If he moves while
I fulfill the pressure, he will sink the blade
into his jugular. I am dreaming this.

II

I am dreaming this. I hold the blade laid
in the rot of the wound it made. The one blade
that can be a balm pouring into that wound
as it cuts through to where there is no blood
but a mysterious ore in radiant flow.
The two of us the wound. Our blood still circling
but out to the unfathomable tips of all
dreaming iron and back. The iron laughs.
I wake, and a grotesque, beautiful one
slides out of me and away. Murderer
who removes the blade clean from the fallen neck,
man who walks free, bright as a song in the air,
my father and I gone, a new instrument
of life, the blade buried and lost in his hand.

Aphrodite's Mirror

Robin in the grass, away in the trees,
on a roof with her new-flying babies,
her breast a visible electric charge,
a flung up orange-red disc. My daughter
is eyeing flowers, pilfering a rich handful
to give to her mother. Now as she runs
into a garden where she vanishes,
half a bouquet in her hand, and runs back,
the petal-glow concentrated on her
becomes a deepening show, a bright play
of the essence of copper. She will go
to her mother flower- and copper-dipped
as her mother was when she called her here
to be born and to know the days and nights,
the two of them as full of clear singing
as twin robins. Her flowers her pendant,
her ancient mirror of polished metal,
she moves to and fro displaying herself
and wherever her eyes lead her. Laughing
while light tells its secrets, while it keeps them,
she runs old ways, from garden to garden,
first artefact of her mother and me,
mirror looking at us, with us, past us.

My Daughter and the Geometry of Time

Clear sun, spring wind twisting spray up off waves,
my daughter digging, dropping shovelfuls
of clean sand through a sea-worn opening
in a jutting limb of a driftwood tree,
watching grains fall to an apex of sand
and slide to the widening base. I see
the black glowing around the visible,
the sun, sky, water, beach flat. There are pairs
of hands in each incoming wave tip's froth,
frenzied, fashioning fire and flinging it,
before they fall away, to the grey sand
and into that black. My daughter is two
and I am almost fifty. My mother's
parents' ashes lie where I buried them
in sand a hundred feet or so from here—
I think of them as having gone within
shells that are spheres of time, the radii
three times the one within which I now stand,
innumerable times the one within
which my daughter now stands, her sphere so new
that it is a radiant point, a source
full of her future. When she is the age
I am now, she will remember nothing
of the hour and a half this afternoon
she and I spent together. She will not
ever know the two people I still see
as clearly as any in my present.
When young they courted here in the beach light,
the worn logs and cornered wind their shelter
and secret escape. Their old eyes become
more and more for me the one sphere of time;
whatever my own eyes see, they give me.

Light taking light into its arms. Light, light,
in shell after shell. I dream I allow
my daughter to know more than I have known.
I think I will be here at her margins
when I am gone in the same way those two
are now at my own margins, receding
to the beginning. I will see the froth
travelling circular intricacies
like white flames from the earth's immense hollows,
scooped up by the waters and let go free,
I will see my small daughter gazing back
at me for a moment from where she stands
collecting and pouring the sand, moving
into the future at the speed of light.

Ambleside Beach

Once or twice in late summer I come here
to swim headlong out into the inlet
as far as I can, and return slowly
on my back trying to let my arms
and legs do their work with animal calm
in the metallic purple-green water,
the transparent cold sea ore. I look up
now into rays falling straight down the air
and fitting the sea, and see the glitter
and melt of the sun, the nickels and dimes
that my grandmother would place in our hands
the nights she visited us and spun spells.
When she had left I would swallow a coin
I half-believed would continue to shine
bright within me like her story. She would
conjure them up for us right on the spot,
though the one about her brother who swam
out from this beach and got caught in the rip
tide, and ended up in a rescue boat,
she put together with drama and flair
from real events of the past. And the one
about her father who brought her mother,
herself and her sister here from far, far
away and built a shack, a makeshift home
to live in on this shore where one evening
we stood in a quiet place in the sand
beyond the touch of the tides and buried
the contents of her urn. Now I swim here,
and now I bring my two-year-old daughter
here to play. While she stays with her mother,
I swim out. My heart muscle strong for now,
beating steady within the sea's rhythm,
I go out and back, I go out and back,

riding my heart and the tide, and the sea
cups me beneath the high sun's deep dazzle.
I remember when I was very young
my grandmother held my face in her hands.
I have her first photographs—few alive
would recognize who the girl was but me.
I swim out to see myself cup my child's
face in my hands and feel for a moment
my grandmother is there as a small girl.
I look straight up, I hear myself saying
Never leave me, the sun pouring ashes
and the sea washing them across my eyes.

Gas

Gas twists in the pupils of the blue eyes,
fastens the backbone to the basket base,
seizes the entrails and crumples the face.
He tries to smile, watery-eyed, staring,
between his grimaces. His cries come fast,
a tiny bird's trill. Breast milk his mother
produces for him as the one true food,
his mouth draws in and his digestive tract
rejects as it drags him down its hooked path.
The flesh nails him to nothing. Even now
my father is here. I want this infant
to fight my father for me. He knows it.
Flesh I helped give him, essence I passed on
to him, holds the father, anger riding
in the ageless sperm. He is filtering
through himself what I filtered through myself,
forbears, human, animal, mineral,
molecular, purifying it
to spirit as he is able. Giving himself
to the invisible. Anger in him.
Anger in my father while he views me
through the eye metal. My son howls, the howl
owns his breath. I cradle him. He closes
his eyes, his mouth set tight, while my father
and my father's father grimace and grit
their teeth within him. He writhes, this small one,
a question he asks returning to him
as himself, all pulsing answer, question,

beyond his comprehending. The body
attempting to digest itself. Hunger
in him instructs him to eat a god. Now
he will turn it into a stink. The god
will hurt him and he will fight it, sweet boy,
six weeks old, toothless, the anger in him,
the death in the gas, the death in the flesh,
with the heaven in living flailing hands.

Iron, a Summary

Train-wheel iron ringing in the rain. Gulls and crows
opening throats that utter their own metal on metal.
Construction roar. Cranes, excavators and drills. Clouds,
concentrated and low, flow with ore and alloy.
The ringing floats up from the shore through the stillness
in the chambers of the air between the raindrops
to vibrate my daughter's eardrums, to touch
at her brow, her cheek, and the soft curls on her head.
The black metal of the crows' wing feathers
brush against her within the ringing, the grey and white
metal of the gulls' wing feathers. The cries
of the birds cross and echo between the inlet
and the mountain. The sound of the train wheels
on a long curve rolls through the bowels of the birds.
The cold edge of the spinning playground ride
scrapes and cuts my daughter's lip in the morning
in the lathe-cut air and she cries, and as soon forgets,
and cries again to keep on playing. *I'm making a train,*
she sings out later, one coloured block after another
along the front room floor. *With seats to sit on.*
Wheel after wheel continues grinding along rails.
The wheels of this other iron turn and show
the rainbows in black wings, the rush of creeks
and waterfalls in grey and white wings. These wheels ring
where the roads go through the insatiable
deep gorge of the human heart from cruelty to mercy,
through the shut furnace of the human face
from jealousy to pity, through the iron of the human dress
from secrecy to peace, and through a fiery forge
from human terror to love. The three-year-old
in brilliant boots splashes through and shatters the metal
of puddles and traces her circle of laughter,
desire clear and new and relentless as the sun and rain.

The Praise Tree

I

Gusts run through the sapling and it shivers and sways,
the leaves lift delicate green, glittering silver,
settle shadow-dark, lift green and silver again,
and the tree is an actress on a stage,
swooning, flinging her hands to the sky. In this play
the bodily motion is beyond measurement
and the speech beyond hearing, it is all the tree's
single intricate electric charge and flow. The sorrow
in this one in the lead role so full of finding,
and of being found, the joy so full of searching,
the leaves are castanets she clicks while wind
undresses her of matter, dresses her in spirit, undresses
and dresses her again many times every minute
as in a wedding dance of the visible and invisible.

II

Because of a chance wind and chance open window
near a well-travelled street, I have become an audience,
the young actress is familiar to me, and the tall tree,
I understand now, is the small potted tree that vanished
from my grandmother's room in the care centre
while she lay in the hospital and we combed out
her long hair and spoke into her ear, telling her
that it was all right, she could let go. The tree's leaves flash
and they flaunt her senses though her old life is gone,
and she is in a play again circa 1930—
it is a play she could never have acted in until now,
though it was always within the play of her life,
and she is alive in the role and cannot know it, as the tree
cannot know she is the way it lives in the wind.

The Aeschylus Rock

Fresh corpse of a baby gull
splayed against a shore rock.
Feathers, guts, skin case, stain,
the sections of the skeleton
like parts of a pictograph,
neck, skull, eye hole, keel,
ribs, ilium, wing bones, claws,
thing that had not flown long
dropped by an eagle or hawk.

The tide will find it in an hour
and take what is left of it,
but for now the bones manacle
the carcass to the dry rock
while the shore rats run out
of nests to get at it. Sunlight
embraces it. The thief of fire
deep within the rock drinks
and eats it and lives forever.

Acknowledgements

Some of the poems in this book first appeared in the following publications:

A Verse Map of Vancouver (Anvil Press, 2009, Ed. George McWhirter)—"When the Big Hand Is on the Starfish"

Arc—"Men Fixing a Roof in the Rain"; "My Daughter and the Seagull's Cry"

The Fiddlehead—"Burrard Inlet Ships"; "The Envelope"; "Greenness"; "The Man Who Sleeps in Cemeteries"; "The Work of the Creek"; "The Rain Bush" (Ralph Gustafson Prize Winner, 2009)

Global Poetry Anthology—Montreal International Poetry Prize 2011 (Vehicule Press, 2012, Eds. Valerie Bloom, Stephanie Bolster, Frank M. Chipasula, Fred D'Aguiar, Michael Harris, John Kinsella, Sinéad Morrissey, Odia Ofeimun, Eric Ormsby, and Anand Thakore)— "Aluminum Beds"

The Literary Review of Canada—"Lead"

The Malahat Review—"Blade"
Maple Tree Literary Supplement—"The Praise Tree"; "Rain Wolf, West

Coast Trail"; "Lost Rain Casting of a Deer"

The New Quarterly—"Andean Flute"

Poems from Planet Earth (Leaf Press, 2013, Eds. Yvonne Blomer and Cynthia Woodman Kerkham)—"The Aeschylus Rock"

Poet to Poet Anthology (Guernica Editions, 2012, Eds. Julie Roorda and Elena Wolff)—"The Oldest Rock in the World"

Rocksalt: An Anthology of Contemporary BC Poetry (Mother Tongue Publishing, 2008, Eds. Mona Fertig and Harold Rhenisch)—"Nest of the Swan's Bones"

subTerrain Vancouver 125 Special Issue—"Burrard Inlet Ships"

The Winnipeg Review—"River Rainbow"; "Playing With Stones"

My thanks to everyone at Harbour Publishing, and to Silas White, editor *par excellence.*

Russell Thornton is the author of several collections of poetry, among them *House Built of Rain* (Harbour, 2003), which was a finalist for the Dorothy Livesay Prize (BC Book Prizes) and the ReLit Award, and *The Human Shore* (Harbour, 2006). His poetry has appeared widely in Canadian literary journals, and in anthologies such as *Rocksalt: An Anthology of Contemporary BC Poetry, Open Wide A Wilderness: Canadian Nature Poems*, the *Montreal International Poetry Prize 2011 Global Poetry Anthology*, and *Best Canadian Poetry in English 2012*. He won the League of Canadian Poets National Contest in 2000 and *The Fiddlehead* magazine's Ralph Gustafson Poetry Prize in 2009. He has lived in Montreal, Aberystwyth, Wales, and Salonica, Greece. He now lives where he was born and grew up, in North Vancouver.